Poetry Diversified
2015
A Human Experience Anthology

Compiled by Lucinda Clark

P.R.A. Publishing
Poetry Matters Project Ltd.
Martinez, GA

Poetry Diversified 2015: A Human Experience Anthology
Copyright © 2015 PRA Publishing

All rights reserved

No part of this book may be reproduced or transmitted by any means, electronic or mechanical, including photocopying, recording, or by any information storage and retrieval system, without permission from the publisher.

ISBN: 978-1-941416-06-8 paperback
ISBN: 978-1-941416-07-5 electronic book
LCCN: 2015931564

PRA Publishing
P.O. Box 211701
Martinez, GA 30917
www.prapublishing.com
Book Design and Cover by Joe Tantillo

Printed in the United States

This book is dedicated to
Maya Angelou
April 4, 1928–May 28, 2014

Contents

Middle School Winners 2013–2014

Time	Gabriella Meerwarth	2
Take Me Back	Caitlyn Duffie	4
Our Kingdom	Tamara Sato	5
The Edge	Emily Knutson	7
Dear Innocence	Graeme Horton	8
The Dungeon Master's Call	Sami Townsend	9
Memories	Min Su Kim	12
My Grandfather	Zackary Kimmel	14
Gone	Gabby Barrido	16
Alone	Juliana Saxe	18
Bullied	Syler Stanfford	19
Regret	Ashlyn Felton	20

High School Winners 2013–2014

Don't Forget What You Believe In	Emma Kane	22
Skinner Box	Lucy Zhou	24
Tremors	Aletheia Wang	25
Immobility on the Mortal Roads	William Kuzia	27
Yesterdays	Joshua Newman	28
2014-03-31-731	Olivia Zhao	31
Pretty	Maria Davila	33
Sheet Music	Dalia Ahmead	36
Rust Belt	Zachary de Stefan	37
Figure 8	Christell Roach	39
I Am Sitting Alone in the Dark	Gabrielle Walters	42
This Life	Kay Ann Henry	43
Murder of Crows	Isabella York	44
Reservation was Our Demise	Kaitlyn Graham	46
Breathless	Mariah Bowman	48

Adults Winners 2013–2014

Good Night Friends	Jennifer Fenn	50
Young Means Forever Unchanging	J.C. Elkin	51
The Trouble with Genealogy	Caroline Zarlengo Sposto	53
Poetic Interpretation of 'Portrait of a Man with a Book'	Stephen Joseph	54
Get Me Some Flowers	Kendall Driscoll	56
Angels with Sledgehammers	Carmen Colado	58
The Loss of a Child	Steven Brooks	59
Christmas	Haitham Al-Twaijri	60
I am Linwood Kendrick or Current Resident	Meg Eden	62
Absent	Karin Tinkel	63
The Things We Didn't Care to Keep	Terrance Daye	64
Cooking Lesson	Ellen Thea	66
A Fracture Marks the Place	Sarah Dansie	67
My Plain and Simple Love	Katherine King	68
Amiri's Revolution	Krystal Valentine	70
My Mother Has No Teeth	Jennifer Lowers	72
Celestial Pursuit	Leah Smith	73
The Bridge	Caren Stewart	74
Warning Label	Cait Cox	77
If We Knew	Mike Wilson	79

Senior Winners 2013–2014

Do You Know Me?	Daniel George	81
The Diagnosis	Ruth Merriman	83
An Artist Remembered	Roger Brock	84
Little Things	Joan Lacombe	86
Father	Mark Littleton	88
The Tale of Emmett Till	Gordon Smith	90
Out of the Wild	David M. Harris	92
Weight	Joan Cannon	93
Yesterday	Sarah Bailey	94
Assassins in Time	Nancy Culp	96
Loved and Cared	Carmen Ruelas Von Tickner	98
I Am A Poem	Jerome E. Howard	99
The Tally of Time	Robert B. Roberson	100

Middle School Winners
2013–2014

Time
Gabriella Meerwarth

A deep blush rushing to your cheeks
How quickly it appears,
Yet how slowly it vanishes

Deadlines,
How far away they may seem,
Yet how quickly they arrive

Just as one season passes to the next,
How long,
Demanding
Oppressive,
We wait,
And yet,
With a photo album on the table,
I think,
It must have been just yesterday.

Months,
Seasons,
Years,
A phasing moon floating above each lifetime,
A ticking,
Thumping clock,
Constant in the thoughts of each soul

And time manipulates us,
Distorted in our minds,
Time goes by slowly,
As a cloud does
Across

The SkyTime goes by recklessly,
Flashing through our eyes.

Time,
With its wanderlust,
Sees our in-betweens,
The unsatisfactory moments,
That we wish had never happened,
And

The moments that trigger your crooked grin
Each moment,
Divided by seconds,
Each hopeless,
Each hopeful,
Each tragically beautiful second,
Passes away

Time sees it all,
A span of infinity.

And I've discovered that time,
Each second,
Tends to not get the credit that it deserves.

It erratic pace,
It's changing current

Time is our enemy.
Yet,
With it's understanding silence,
It's prominent healing,
Time is our friend.

Take Me Back
Caitlyn Duffie

I refuse to continue forward
in the days where slips-ups are permanent,
where grass grows brown and flowers wilt,
where confusion is the author
of every ripped up page in my book.

I want to go back to when I waited
quietly under the wooden table
for the man who bore gifts.

Rewind the clock. Let it tick
at the moments when my smile
covered my face, when my parents'
words were my manual for life.

Allow me to trace familiar steps,
to find that one day when happiness
reigned, when innocence was my cover story.

I want to revisit the days
when everything was kosher
in such an imperfect society,
when my mother told me
"Everything rising of the sun
brings forth another chance to shine,"
and it came to pass.

Take me back to the days
when I was the princess
in this fairytale.

Our Kingdom
Tamara Sato

Out I marched, Ready for the world and all of its adventures,
Only to be run over by the sound of early mornings.
Three, two, One I get up, and start Again.
This time, Defiantly rising,
With my Fist held Triumphantly in the air.

Determined, like a baby learning
To walk for the First time.
I Paste a bright smile on my face
And become a Mountain,
Too magnificent and Breathtaking and Strong
To be Blown down by the wind.

Up, I waddle, to My very own Kingdom
Beyond the Faded blue house and the
Musty, moldy brick Wall,
Where Once again, I am the Ruler
Of every dandelion and blade of grass
For feet in Every direction around.

I slide down the grass on a Makeshift sled
Gaining speed, and excitement, and
A Wide grin, which Spreads slowly across my face.
I stop...
And laugh Uncontrollably,
Accidentally lying on the squishy grass,
The Muddy Grass, covering myself in it,
Like a Dirty blanket of Love.

I'm having the time of my life here,
Me in my brown, wet clothes, with my

Flowery friends all around.
Them, a boy comes from
Out of the blue,
His eyes Wide with curiosity.

I become Stiff and Protective,
For I am The Ruler,
The Top of the Food Chain,
The Hero.

But he, with his innocent, lonely, young eyes,
Begging.
I am Lost in confusion, Torn apart,
For how can a bear Challenge
The order of Dominance?

But kindness takes over, and I give him
Half of my cardboard, and half of my Trust,
And We ride down the hill of Wonders:
Me, and the person I call "Brother."

Out We March, ready for the world and all of its Adventures,
Racing to our Castle,
Behind the dilapidated house
And the Old Brick wall,
Where we are the Rulers:
Together

The Edge
Emily Knutson

On the edge
of darkness
A vast field
of velvety comfort
Calling

So seductively it taunts
its luxury bends your will
falling in its arms
the demons that lurk about
they take you
as you become vulnerable
in the comforting arms of darkness

At home in its embrace
At peace when running away
When free you long for its shelter
When entangled you long to be released

Forever on the edge
Unsure of what is to come

Dear Innocence
Graeme Horton

You came to me,
When I was born into this world
and I was only able to keep you for so long.
I have done shameful things and for that,
I lose you.
It was a privilege to know that I possessed you
and that I deserved you,
but now
you are a dream that never comes true.
It is somewhat freeing to not have you anymore,
it allows me not to worry about losing you.
Few people retain you for the entirety of their lives,
I am not one of the exceptions.
I bid you farewell on your journey to another soul to make a
    home,
and I feel happy knowing that you will be in the care of
    someone else.
Someone worthier than me.

The Dungeon Master's Call
Sami Townsend

Nerd is a proud word,
forged by Dr. Suess,
and released to the world,
to run rampant, loose
like a wild goose.
It jumped into our movies,
caught fire in our media,
and duct-taped itself
to our slang,
our vocab.
Taken by those who gang-bang
and sewn to the collars of us
whose books are thrown,
whose pencils are snapped,
glasses disgraced,
and Legolas binders defaced.
Here's a newsflash:
We rule the world!
Our title is a battle cry,
echoed at every ComicCon,
every LOTR marathon,
heard in every light saber clash.
Every orc's skull bashed
is a step closer to a victory banquet,
our Iron Throne.
Who do you think makes computers compute?

That's right, us.
We sit on a boat,
gliding over the world,
writing the codes,
with all the variables, the parentheses,

the semicolons.
We dip our fingers over the edge.
Our hands glide through the colored numbers and words,
fingers gently arranging, brushing the codes
that keep the world afloat.
And if I've lost you here,
you are no nerd.
In case you haven't heard,
we have standards, a code.
Welcome to the nerd herd,
the most exclusive group in town.
Our members only jackets
have TARDIS stitched into the back,
'cause if it's one thing we have plenty of,
it's Time And Relativity,
and one thing we know is Dimensions In Space.
Let the horn of Gondor
call all Whovians, Bronies, Ringlets, Star Wars fans,
lovers of anything that travels the stars,
of anything that labels you "nerd".
Stand up!
Stand together!
Fight!
Pick up your swords, your lightsabers,
your sonic screwdrivers,
and face those who disgrace us.
And if you don't know who I am,
I'll tell you!

I'm the dungeon master,
the leader of the nerd herd,
controller of D'n'D fate.
And though one may not simply walk into Mordor,
we can all stand and fight.
Fight for our memes,
For Narnia!
For all nerds!
May the force be with you.

Memories
Min Su Kim

Memories
Swirling lightly like snowflakes,
Completely oblivious to the chaos in the world.
Lost history scavenged up by photos.
By preservations
That were used to protect these fragile objects.
Turbulent pasts erased,
Happy times forgotten,
Only to be revived and sought out by distant memories.
Memory
A light that burns either dimly or brightly,
Shadowed by sheets and layers of time.
They race against time,
Lapsing back
Only to be rekindled,
Or neglected.
Time dims the memory,
Fogging it over with years of newer ones.
They are footsteps long vanished,
Leaving ghosts of itself
Unseen traces of itself
Behind.
It is this ghost from the past that can be a path to future,
Reminding us who we used to be.

Who we must be in a second,
A minute,
An hour,
A day,
A year,
And a lifetime.
They shock
They burn,
Bring desire and sorrow.
Yet, the weight of present and future depend on the power of memories,
So how would we learn without it?

My Grandfather
Zachary Kimmel

My Grandfather
My grandfather
Is cold in his bones
A heart of ice
A frostbitten soul
My grandfather
is broken glass
graffiti and smoke
rising into the empty heavens
My grandfather
is a yellow star
with the word Jude
embroidered with hate
My grandfather

Is a train
Carrying a heavy load
of human cargo
to the ends of the earth
My grandfather
is a camp
piles of humans
a march through snow
a bottomless pit
endless night
I am a grandchild of the Holocaust
One of many
But there are many who are not here
Stolen
Every breath we take
Reminds us of the millions
Stolen

The gas did not fill our lungs
It fills our eyes with tears
The fire did not burn our flesh
It burns a hole in our hearts
We did not wear the yellow star
But still we feel its weight.

Gone
Gabby Barrido

The moon—
Just a large grey rock,
Nothing special,
Hovering, doing nothing,
Just a light
When everything is dark,
Just a guide
When all seems lost,
Just a magnet
Creating towering waves,
Just a leader
Of all the water.
The moon seems to be useless,
But is so significant.
Does the moon get lonely
Sitting in the vast, empty sky,
Watching over everything,
Staying in the background?

Does the moon get sad
Not being noticed,
Just walked by,
Not so much as a single glance?
It stays strong
But can only take so much.
The moon only shows one side
Hiding behind a façade,
Showing off a glamorous image
For everyone to see
The dark side of the moon is beautiful
But is too scared to show the world.
What if if the moon disappeared one day?
Maybe no one will notice.

Maybe the moon is already gone,
But no one cared enough to realize.

Alone
Juliana Saxe

When people say
I like being alone

Or

I'm a loner and proud of it
are they trying to make
people break down walls
to see who will stay
to find their true friends
or are they saying
I don't like being hurt
I've been hurt before
please don't hurt me

Bullied
Syler Stanfford

I look down at the ground
only to see my legs
covered in bruises
and my arms
covered in scars
why do you not like me
what did I do
all I ever wanted
was to be treated like a friend
with respect and love
until the end
everyday i sit and wonder
what it would be like to have another
another person here with me
to live in my life with care and friendship
I only wish my dreams were true to
finally have a friend who cares but i know that won't happen
I sit and wonder about my options and come to see
no one wants me
as a friend
as a person
or as anything
I see the pills on the counter
seeing i have no future
I open the lid and take
one last moment to think
about that one last dream,
 to think about if anyone
really cares about me,
I can see me gone, no one cares
I guess i have nothing to lose
so to all the people that dont like me alive
i never meant to make you mad
cause all i wanted
was for you to be my friend,
I hope I made you happy
cause i wont bother you again,
cause you'll never see me again.
Bye

Regret
Ashlyn Felton

I sit in a cold, dark corner,
Alone.
Thinking about what I've done,
I start thrashing my head side to side
Trying to forget about the past.
I regret it,
Thinking about what could have happened if I didn't do it.
Maybe we would be together having fun,
Or maybe we would just be talking about random subjects,
Laughing at each other's stupid jokes.
But what's done is done, and I can't change it.
My trembling hands clutch my head,
The iciness seeping into my face.
I lift my head up,
Enough to look at all of the objects that remind me of the time I spent with you.
The pictures we took together, the crafts we made, the presents and little knick knacks
that you gave me,
They all make me think of everything we did together.
All of a sudden, the memories come flooding back to me.
I shouldn't have done it.

High School Winners
2013–2014

Don't Forget What You Believe In
Emma Kane

I believe that there is too much to believe in,
that these thoughts lead to confusion,
that these confusing thoughts appear in our brains for a reason,
and everything happens for a reason.
Love isn't believable;
in movies and television shows, love appears to be,
but it isn't. I cant define love, so to me, it is unbelievable.
I believe in love songs though,
I believe that music heals our hearts
and holds our hands through rough times.
Like my mom. I believe in her and she believes in me.
Like a beautiful song, she holds my hand when life gets hard.
My mom tells me what she believes in:
she believes in me.
She believes that one must work hard for their dreams and
aspirations.
I believe in success,
and I believe in sitting on my couch and doing nothing.
Money, money, money. I don't need a lot of it but its nice to
    have.
I don't believe in failure,
unless it's handed to me on the test I look last week.
I believe in unicorns, aliens and mermaids.
I think kids are the biggest believers but I don't believe in them;
they grow up to become non-believers.
I do believe in non-believers though;
they believe in having no beliefs.
I don't believe in worrying, unless it's about my future.
I believe we live our lives less as we worry more,
but I don't live by it.

I think I got the worrying gene from my grandma;
she worries more than anyone I know,
but she is the best person I know,
next to my mom.
I don't like goodbyes but I do believe in closure.
I can't make the same mistake twice.
I will stand by her bed and hold her hand if she needs it.
I didn't go to hospital for my grandpa.
I wish I could tell my grandma this,
but I don't believe in crying.
I believe in bottling up my emotions and volcanoes.
I believe that there's so much to believe in
and so much to learn, so we forget everything.
I forget what I write down until I reread it.

Skinner Box
Lucy Zhou

Their bloated bodies waddle around me,
their beady eyes hawkish and black
against the sunset. I extend a palm
to the pigeons, crumb here and there
less for the deed, more for the sight. Watching
these pigeons line up in a row, I am reminded
of Skinner Box-- how easy it is to tempt another
into submission. The palm resting on my shoulder
suddenly feels heavy, just living iron bound
in flesh. I think of the apple that feels compelled
towards its roots. I think of the roots
that strangle its very seeds. The individual fingers are
as penetrating as the tree of life itself, a fatherly love
bound in complications as fine as threads.
So here I am, hand feeding beak, a circus of pigeons beneath my
    feet,
with the palm of another cradling my shoulder,
his eyes critical and silent. The man with the palm and eyes
like a reflection hushes me quiet, but all I hear
is the cawing of pigeons. A new seed blooms in my ear
as terrifying as a revelation--animale or kin,
I cower underneath the ringmaster.

Tremors
Aletheia Wang

His fingers sweep the piano keys
just how they always did
but the melody is different now,
strangled in its urgency, a riot
of leisure and death and liquor
that fizzed its way into the masterpiece
he had been phrasing, and now
it is impossible for the devastated iron
to be extracted from the ore of the song.
Light hits the ginger bottles, straddling
his earlier time as a concert pianist
and now,

the fissure a keyboard robbed of notes.
His mottled fingers still flutter,
but they move on their own.
He plays in places his younger self
would rather have died than enter,
honing a single story on stage each night.
He plays slow mazurkas and thinks of
a couple dancing the murders of courtship
to those songs centuries ago.
A woman glides along in admirable time,
her dress a flame in a cave, then falls.

Later, when the drinks set in, he feels the ribbed roads tangling
    in the wind.
Rain sings on cobblestones
his feet topple over; its music holds
no recognition. Clear blossoms foam
on the pathway to his front door, spinning
in hairline scrapes on a piano's cover.

He cannot sleep. His life chases before him,
dropping like the grimy coins strangers
condescend to throw.
His fingers float, borne anew.
The garden shakes behind his smoke.

Immobility on the Mortal Roads
William Kuzia

Here is where I stand.
There are two paths before me.
I know what I demand.
I don't know which road is for me.

The one I've been on is long and worn.
It pains my feet to tread here.
The one to my side is dark and lorn.
The pain of that road is my fear.

I fear I may never take the step,
and this road will scar my feet.

But if I stumble on forever,
when will the two roads meet?

Should I linger and endure this soil?
If I leave then will I wake?
Here is where I stand, unmoving,
until a choice I make.

Yesterdays
Joshua Newman

Life is filled with colors
Of tomorrow and today.
Today's deep hues
Of greens and blues,
And tomorrows shades of grey.

Today creates sweet moments
The memories we will find,
When today has gone,
And life moved on,
And this moment is left behind.

Today is the father of progress,
The breeding ground of thought.
It gives the mind
A chance to find
The achievement it has sought.

And yet today is but a moment,
Slipping ever so quickly by,
It comes each day,
Then fleets away
As a storm cloud in the sky.

For today cannot last long,
As it comes and goes so fast.
It dissolves away
Into yesterday,
And today fades into past.

Now tomorrow buds with promise.
And the thrill of the unknown.
It is the time and day
When plans are laid.
And the place where dreams are grown.

The future holds such wonder;
With life's mysteries untold.
It brings a silent thrill
While at the Maker's will,
All the scenes of life unfold.

But the future is a myth.
A promise ever unfulfilled.
So close each day,
Yet so far away,
Each tomorrow distant still.

Each today is far too short
To spend it waiting for the next.
And awaiting sorrow
On the morrow
Can be hardly called the best.

Every future moment
Turns out to be today.
And then in time
They both, we find,
Turn into yesterday.

Such is the way of the world.
Such the will of Fate.
Each moment spent in reverie
Spawns more and greater memories
The longer that we wait.

And perhaps it's just as well that way
For though reality is grand,
Don't ever hesitate
To contemplate
What you can never understand.

7:31 A.M.
Olivia Zhao

This morning I tripped
And saw the sunrise.

My coffee spilled from my thermos
Upended on its side
And the fragrant liquid spewed out,
Steaming as it hit
The cool, gray sidewalk.

This morning my coffee spilled
And I saw the sunrise.

Knees, chest, and chin all met
The cool, gray sidewalk
And one whole millisecond passed before
Everything all over
Just hurt.

This morning my body met the ground
And I met the sunrise.

I rolled over and
For a few painful seconds
I just lay on the walk
And stared up at the sky
Like a bug stuck on its back.

This morning I looked up
And saw the beauty of the sunrise.

Most mornings are scripted
So that I roll out of bed to dress then
Pour my thermos of coffee then

Run out to my car then slam the door and
Drive west.
Most mornings I drive west
And never see the sunrise.

But laying on my back I looked
Above the shadows
Cast by cold steel building edges
And saw scarlet and orange hues
Warmer than the rushing breeze.
This morning my schedule halted at 7:31
As I looked east to the sunrise.

It was a whole new world.

Pretty
Maria Dávila

Last night I:
plucked my eyebrows
straightened my hair
painted my nails
stayed up until three in the morning
searching the wonders of Cosmo
and surfing the internet for beauty tips
"how to fake fuller eyebrows
in seconds" "anything is possible
with a wig and a dream" What?
I: looked for the perfect make-up
to match my skin complexion
because it's not enough to be God's
original creation,
traded integrity for security
and called it love
looked for a celebrity to look up to
because being me was not
good enough and Miley Cyrus
has bleached her eyebrows
news that traveled the nation
while I cry and tell myself,
"be patient, be patient."
This morning I:
put on my eyeliner
made my lashes artificial with mascara
painted my lips and powdered
my cheeks but I:
was still not what I wanted to be
was still not pretty
and I wasn't the only one to know
because all the girls told me so

This morning I:
looked again into my worst enemy
the mirror that might've lied to me
because when you're a teen
every mirror you look into is so mean
meaner than the girls who bullied me
or the guys who took my self-esteem
or my dad who drenched me
with insults so I:
abandoned my innocence
became bitter
open to all sorts of abuse
that became so hard to refuse
and the truth is
I wanted more
wanted more than
pick-up lines and beady eyes
more than men shouting vulgarities
more than what I was
I wanted to be more.
This morning I:
heard myself whispering affirmations
digging out every bit of information
put into my fifteen year old head
jumped on my bed
because I was not a reincarnation
but a lab rat
let out of her cage

and I'll never forget when I heard
myself say "no" over and over again
but he wouldn't listen
when he pinned me down
and took the tiny bit of innocence
that had come back and I:
closed down
loved God more than me
loved music more than me
loved clothes and food more than me
love him more than me but I:
walk about all hips and lips
giving in because what else
can become of me? I:
was still not pretty.

Sheet Music
Dalia Ahmead

When my grandfather held me,
his body was a broken piano.
His smile curved into the turn-
pins of his hollow cheeks, caving
into those tunes we handpicked,
humming, beneath date trees.

I saw his heart quivering
on a tight-rope above my palms,
the lyrics creeping into the cracks
between my fingerprints.

He always told me that
if he were to die, he wanted birds
to perch themselves on his arms,
spread their arrow-thin wings
across his veins and stain their talons
with his blood.

We once made playgrounds
out of grand pianos, where I'd hoped
he'd find the song—lyrics composed
of his obituary—tucked underneath the keys,
pressed into a music box. My grandfather
promised he'd never forget the tune
he'd grasped in his hands
because while he was the voice
I was his sheet music.

Rust Belt
Zachary de Stefan

Walks down those halls
were lessons in lung capacity;
anything to keep from breathing
in the air, stale and dry like old
bones --

if you were lucky, the pounding
in your head would drown out
the screaming woman
who'd claw at the walls in search
of nothing and everything
at once,

and there she sat,
eyes averted, facing the city
smeared outside the rain-slick
glass, and we'd bend down
in silent observation
of the woman we hardly
recognized, tucked deep
beneath the purpled skin
and the mane of hair that still
carried the faint scent
of lemons that Mom mistook
for hope

She said once that her Papa
had toiled away on train tracks
for twenty years in that city
of gristle and steel;
he's been buried up
on the north side of Dutch Hill

for half a century now,
and still those veins snake
across the ancient streets
like they'd been laid
just yesterday

People never go away,
she told me, not really;
and then -
still grinding your teeth?
You got that from me,
you know

How's Tiger doing?
I hope you've stopped
feeding him twice a day,
you know what Dr. Jacobi
said Good, good, good

I want you to know
that I look for you often,
whenever we take a ride
down I-80, and I think
I see you now more than ever,
in those gutted barns that line
the highway, in the rolling hills
burned out like candlewick,
and I'm scared,
Grandma, because Mom
can't bend down anymore.

Figure 8
Christell Roach

I walk off my nerves with my body feeling like a pitch-pipe.
This must be what is was to feel the humming in your
    instrument,
once it reached its final note in a concerto.

When I dance with my flags, my body becomes a physical
    ministry,
a wordless art form, prayer in motion.

My arm extensions are drenched. I hold the colored fabric and
    think
of how moments ago I was flagging my speech.

I choreographed with daffodils crawling into the crevices of my
    hands.

Now I sit with the organza fabric in my lap, and I look around
    me:

The evening sun is sitting cross-legged, eyes half shut,
watching the nocturnal orchestra set itself up.

Monuments are being desecrated tonight. Again.
A woodpecker is constructing;

a skin is being peeled into a transposition,
an owl is psalming itself into a tree,
a blossom out of season is dismantling herself.

The sky is watercolor bleeding into pictograms.
The conductor is dressed in a different phase tonight.

If I dance for her, if I wave these baton-like instruments,
then the al fine of my concerto will get caught
in the citrus trees up the road.

There is no room for my flags in this scene. I wish to pick up
my silver flags, and begin to connect the dots above,

the unstrung night-lights in the sky, as the conductor spindles
the trees about her path. But I cannot dance without a time-
 signature.

For a moment I am an almanac with no tercet
to cover my lips, an unchained melody suspending the violist.

I tiptoe into art the same way the conductor sneaks closer;
a dancer with textile for her expression.

I whispered to a siren that I am an interpretation,
and then ran into the corners of her mouth, trailing my flags
to find the stitches that held the triads on her tongue.

Rain drains the heavens, but my ears are blind to bitter water,
and I tell Dawn that I am dew enough to keep her away.

The wind is surging. An unanswered question. My eyes
are deaf to the vibrato shaking the trees so violently.

Grasshoppers arpeggio through the blanket of night,
waltzing to the conductor's tempo. If I could teach them to flag,
then I would have a sea of contortions around me..

I am lost, but not lost; I am frozen in fresco. I am tenuto
with no note-value, movement without tire, epilogue with no
 story.

I sit on tear-drops of poetry, tracing my flag like it is the wing
of an injured blue jay; and I wait for my sun

to tickle the grass hello, and for the crickets
to grab hold of their stars again and re-tune their instruments,
so that I might have music enough to dance again.

I Am Sitting Alone in the Dark
Gabrielle Walters

I'm sitting alone in the dark

On the black and white sheets with my phone in my hand.
It's 10:23 on the second day of a new year
and I'm already breaking all my promises.
I promised myself I wouldn't lie,
but now I'm telling you I won't forgive you
even though I'm already wondering
how we'll be able to clean up the messes
you seem to be programmed to make.
I promised I wouldn't spend my time on someone
who doesn't deserve a millisecond of it,
yet the way you look when you're confused
and the scent you carry have crossed my mind
for the thousandth and one time today.
I promised not to
care,
yet here I am wondering if science can explain
the weight in my chest,
how I'm able to physically feel missing you.

This Life
Kay Ann Henry

This Life
This life is such a mystery
There's so much in sight that we don't see
Sometimes I wonder what's my purpose on this earth
Life can be such a mirth
As if the joy that welcomes birth

This life is complete actuality
We know who we are but not what be may be
Pressure is passion's poison and we get a dose of it everyday
But life is about living for today
You have to take chances or your life will never change
You can't direct the winds but you sure can adjust the sails

This life can be tricky, try not to be compelled
Opportunity never knocks twice but there is always the doorbell
You can never forget but always forgive
Cause the past has a way of holding you captive
Ability can get you far but it takes character to keep you there
Nature can be so cruel, predators are everywhere

This life has so many dimensions
Or maybe it's just a battle of perception
But what we think is not what we always see
Our expectations are so different from reality
But optimism is like the sun and doubt is the rain
Life is only beautiful for those who know how to celebrate the pain.

Murder of Crows
Isabella York

The demon of selfishness has risen, killing empathy.
Arising to our detriment, destroying beauty.
Ghastly, casting its shadow over purity.
A shift in the mind, that's all it takes.
A freezing wind,
For the widow to stop mourning.
For the bird to sweep over the land and take what he believes is
   rightfully his.
He swallows, the branch snaps.
Faith is not a slim string, connecting the shallow masses

Can you hear it?
Perhaps listen a bit more, the soothing quiet is not as sweet as it
   seems.
The buzz of life, is a fearful wave of greed and lust.
Questing after shadows.
Devotion to a single consciousness.
The chance to devour is no miracle in itself.
There is no such thing as the thought of nothing-
Only the thought of reason.

I can't imagine the snow settling, the fire burning.
I can only see the faults, never the soft minded.
The mind is a maniac, with constant ambitions.
Have the sweet sounds ever been so bright?
The call for empathy is so loud, it's crying, shrieking, screaming!
The man stumbled into pure desolation.
Can I say a miracle is coming?
How can a race lack so much empathy?
I see it dressed up in it's own affairs.
Do you see it?
A plaque of fever sweeps through.
Here comes breakfast, lunch and dinner.
The black dust covers more and more..
The crows perch over their meals, devouring whatever they can find.
Squabbling over carrion.
Murder of Crows.

Reservation Was Our Demise
Kaitlyn Graham

I remember the cloud of delusion
That served as a crown I bore on my naïve head.
I remember the fantastical mirages
And implausible aberrations from my
Typically sorrowful contemplations.
I remember the entrancing moments
When our eyes would meet
Like two lovers distanced by war,
And you would smile like a school boy that just won a frivolous scuffle—
Proud, and the slightest bit relieved.

Isn't it frightening
That the way we felt could be so easily manipulated by the words and actions of those around us?
Isn't it pitiful
That the burning passion that danced between us-
A recital of butterfly ballerinas-
Could diminish until our love was hardly enough to keep either one of us alive?

We had crafted a castle for us to share-
With tall towers and intricate stonework.
We refined this haven-
Stair by stair-
Until our adoration had produced something so perfect there was nothing more to change.

On our darkest day-

When the progressing thunderclouds loomed over our palace-
I watched our walls crumble and fall.
During our darkest hour,
I watched our fortress collapse at the hands of society's
   rainstorm.

Isn't it frightening
That the jewel of our affection was demolished in the midst of a
   single tempest?
Isn't it pitiful
That we both watched it all happen,
And neither of us attempted to stop it?

Breathless
Mariah Bowman

In our dreams
We hike a mountain road at dusk
It is autumn, and the cool air tastes of rain and earth
We tilt our heads back, and the innumerable stars
Paint us small
and alone.
We search for another, search
but cannot find a soul for miles
not one soul for miles.
The sky, the sky
It swallows us whole
And we wake,
gasping
at the eternity of the autumn night

Adult Winners
2013–2014

Good Night Friends
Jennifer Fenn

To all who lost loved ones in the Sandy Hook Massacre

Under winter stars in houses warmed
by scents still lingering from simmering dinners,
children snuggle up to moms and dads,
who read them stories of people being rescued
from dragons, wolves, and evil stepmothers.
They curl up under blankets, dreaming of being the ones to
    rescue their friends, their families, us, from these same
    monsters.
Lights disappear from windos around the town.
Goodnight, moon. Goodnight, stars.

In the morning, they leave their flannel pajamas,
still smelling clean like last night's hot baths, folded under their
    pillows.
The dreams still stir in their kindergarten minds
at breakfast, on the drive to school,
of being celebrated rescuers amid applause, hugs, and
    multitudes of new friends.

But then it rains showers of bullets
too fast for them to shield their teachers,
too fast for them to lead their classes to escape,
to fast for them to run away themselves.
Good night, friends. Good night, teachers.
Good night, little would-be rescuers.

But wait.
It's still only morning

Young Means Forever Unchanging
J.C. Elkin

Of all my ESL students,
Young is the one I can't reach.
No sense of syntax at all.
Random words tumble from him
like poetry magnets, in heaps,
and he's lost most of the verbs.

"Me restaurant eating friends."

Every day is the same.
Holding his paper at length.
Adjusting, wiping bifocals.
Adopting a thoughtful pose.
Copying words like a monk.
Perfecting each faint letter.
Always a question behind.
Sometimes on the wrong page.

Words crowd his mouth like marbles
slipping under his tongue.
I model. He interrupts.
I shush him. Tell him to listen.
Two, three, four times,
"I went out to eat with friends"
until a stranger just might
understand what he says.

One day I ask the whole class,
"What do you say to someone
who's done something nice for you?"

Twenty blank stares reply
in thunderous incomprehension.
Only Young knows the answer,
parroting my exact words
for each of his many gifts
of candy and flowers and fruit.
"Thank you so much," he says.
Good manners are his forte.

That Christmas we celebrate
with an international feast.
The best student speaks for the class.
Gives me a card, a gift,
heartfelt simple thanks.

Then Young, not to be outdone,
stands and recites four words:

"Warm teacher.
　Born teacher."

Now I'm the speechless one.

The Trouble with Genealogy
Caroline Sposto

I equate Sam Spade in his fedora
with people seeking clues about their roots.
Leisure time has followed diaspora
so heritage is one of our pursuits.

Those little things we do online at night
can overtake our concrete lives by day.
a pilgrimage by trans-Atlantic flight,
swabbed specimens for mapping DNA.

With luck, some forebear we track down will be
of an ilk that we consider striking.
How splendid should our own identity
prove us progeny to prince or viking!

We overlook one truth when self-impressed
by bloodlines and official pedigrees,
that hail our surname, heraldry and crest:
fibs grow and ripen on ancestral trees.

For our human race is hot and bothered—
thus, prone to rendezvous with vamp or cad.
Not all babies christened have been fathered
by that old man they grew up calling "Dad!"

Poetic Interpretation of 'Portrait of a Man with a Book'

about 1524, by Francesco Mazzola (1503-1540): Barrister's black book

Stephen Joseph

It is all here in this book of secrets that I hold gently
Tales of woe and agony abound aplenty.

Dark deeds done without a hint of remorse
Crimes of passion and murder most foul of course.

I am neither a scrivener nor a doctor
But rather belong to the Order of Barrister.

In this black book have I presented
All the guilt and sins of leeches I have successfully represented.

Clever legal jargon have I avoided you see
To make plain the heinous acts of vermin I have set free.

Nary a wink do I sleep some nights
Bringing out of jail commoners who have got into knife fights.

Why do you look upon me with contempt and scorn?
One fine day when you least expect it you might blow my legal horn.

Perhaps you consider me somewhat of a pariah
But if you were wrongly accused, I would no doubt be your messiah.

I am not proud of the work that I have done
Believe me, defending murderers is not much fun.

But I carry on in my toxic profession for recompense
Determined to skewer justice in a wasteland called jurisprudence.

Get Me Some Flowers
Kendall Driscoll

Get me some flowers the day you realize I'm not like all the
 other girls in our class of 262 graduates.
You'll find yourself planning out the strategy of how to ask me
 out.
I'll be at my locker, and you'll be there, too, with violets in hand
because you know how they are my favorite since I am named
 after them.

Get me a bouquet of pink roses for prom.
You know how I love their smell, their delicate petals, and their
 aesthetically pleasing appearance.

Show me that you care enough to make this evening memorable.
Do it just for me.

Get me a simple vase full of flowers for our wedding.
Who needs extravagance when simplicity can provide all?
I love you and you love me,
and that's all that will ever matter in the long run of forever.

Get me some carnations and leave them next to the hospital bed while I'm getting my chemo.
Attach a note to the stem of the single violet thrown into the sea of red that says, "You're beautiful,"
even though my hair has fallen out and my skin has blanched to a sickly whitened tinge.
Bone marrow transplants, several hospitalizations, and a diagnosis of terminal cancer can't stop our love.

Get me some flowers the day my body gives out and I am finally at peace.
Place those violets, carnations, and lilies on my gravestone.
Don't say goodbye to me for we always knew that cancer would be my end.
Just get me some flowers for the day we meet again.

Angels with Sledgehammers
Carmen Colado

With every conversation
I'm comfortable enough to spill truths
You chip away at the concrete blocking
my vulnerable from your view
We were mutually raised with emotional distance the standard

It was once considered weakness to speak of feelings much less have them
In shutting down expression our greatest voice became silence no one can judge what remains immobile and violently quiet.

Years behind our bricks led to some sense of control
We thought there was strength in the protection of our walls

But through the concealment of who we fundamentally are inside
We've forgotten ourselves because of so much we hide
There will be someone, somewhere, at some point in your life
Willing just to listen, not seeking to offer advice
They'll be worthwhile because when they're selfless- they mean it
There's no ulterior motive, no gain from your secrets
What they have to give take it at its face value
These people don't come often, they're rare and there's few
These angels, these Samaritans, these golden-hearted friends
Cherish when you find them- they're armed for your defense

The Loss of a Child
Steven Brooks

In better times
There are many words.
But today is the shortest day.
It is a day filled with night.
With voices small and empty,
And incapable of sound.
Where have you gone?
When the sun rose
There was no light.
In darkness
My questions blindly resonated
To and fro, to and fro
Will I be condemned to ask
Until I find an answer?
'Till a clear ray of light
Finds my old eyes,
And penetrates their mist?
My heart is heavy
And yet there are no words,
Though it beats.
Even now love blinds
And I carry you my son
Like the day you were born
But today is the shortest day.

Christmas
Haitham Al-Twaijri

Houses all about me
Are bright and filled with cheer
To celebrate the day of birth
Most joyous of the year.

Siblings, cousins gather,
The air alive with mirth,
Presents neatly wrapped and boxed
And socks above the hearth.

A day of celebration now
With family nestled tight—
I wonder where my family is
And what they dream tonight.

A thousand miles away they sleep;
Their dreams in different words;
I wouldn't know what thoughts they felt
No matter had I heard.

Their lives a different habit,
Their God a different name,
But for my skin, my hair, my face
I'd swear we weren't the same.

My life they've been this far away
And so, for now, they'll be,
But nothing ever can remove
The heart of them that lives in me.

I am my people's person,
The desert's in my blood,

The feet that tread this foreign ground
Ages upon the sand had stood.

Their spirit lies within me—
At least I'm sure it must—
But now a different spirit sings
A song I long to trust.

It sings of smiles and merriment
Of love that knows no end,
It sings of peace, of joy, of life,
Of birth and of the end.

It sings of sweet reunion,
Of family and fate—
Holidays mean most to those
Who cannot celebrate.

I am Linwood Kendrick or Current Resident
Meg Eden

I am Linwood Kendrick, or Current Resident.
I am "& Jane", the appendage afterthought for extended family.
I am that girl getting married.

I am the Only Child, buried in a stone of lineage.
I am the house that has mail returned invalid.
I am an address for a place that no longer exists.

I am a biography from a journal with no name.
I am a poem that is read and misunderstood.
I am my father's chess piece, my mother's novel.

I am mistaken for my chin hairs.
I am the sixth pianist requested only in emergencies.
I am that girl at ballet practice, whose best friend demands,
    What's my surprise for today?

I am God's stapler, no—I am one staple embedded in my
    master's holiness—
and for this I weep in awe and delight.

Absent
Karin Tinkel

Its not enough to be an illusion
a figment of someone's expectations
Present with body absent of mind

Its not enough to be the puppet
A creation of someone's gift
Present with body absent of soul

Its not enough to be the shadow
a shadow of someone's light
Present with body absent of dream

The Things We Didn't Care to Keep
Terrance Daye

I have always admired
a photograph's acute ability to remember.

It's matchless power to capture a simple moment, and to
    eternalize a scene.

There is a picture that I remember
that showed my grandparents on their wedding day.

I never knew them, but I could see that they were happy once,
  and it seemed to me that inside that timeworn Polaroid

the world could have drifted away from them and they would
  still be anchored to the harbor

that rolled quietly in the other's eyes so I longed to be with
  them.

I would rub my fingers across the face of that film

as if just below its surface
lay something meaningful waiting to be uncovered.

For years we would stumble upon that image.

Sometimes with an unexplainable tenderness, at others with an
  acquired tone of indifference.

But every time, with each new discovery we found its edges
  fading, the scene fainting faster
until its image became so unrecognizable that we finally stopped
  looking

and eventually like all the other things
it became lost to us, forgotten in our powerful stride.

Cooking Lesson
Ellen Thea

Fragrant subtlety,
aromatic nuance.
I want to savor each delectable step
of this meandering journey.
A hint of this,
a splash of that,
Sprinkle the spices generously, delicately,
we simmer, low burn,
the occasional stir here and there.
scorching this dish will never do.
Too soon, too often
checking a souffle,
the wishful blooming.
But oh how I dream
that our peripherally watched
unwatched pot
will soon boil over,
riotous, tumultuous bubbles,
steam rising,
our cake will be baked
and I'll lick the icing
off your fingers.

A Fracture Marks the Place
Sarah Dansie

Comes back to you, in sharp familiar ways,
through thick and blackest tar with feathered brush.
A fracture marks the place you laid him down;
soft peat holds fast where other purchase fails.

Comes back to you, delivered by strange hand
to pass you by unmet on shadowed path.
Your drogue still cast, and on such tempest seas
(the likes of her dark winds seek empty sails).

Comes back to you, and weary in his keep,
and holding things, and sleeping still enough
that waking cannot see. A fracture marks
the place. Soft peat held fast. Your purchase failed.

My Plain and Simple Love
Katherine King

Life, like time, slipped by unmarked,
Without tone, without depth, without flavour,
Until he came, my soul revived,
And life was wine to savour.
We spoke of all and nothing,
Of beginnings and of ends,
No words of love were uttered,
It sufficed that we were friends.
We stood as one with hands entwined to face the world
    together,
And I knew no doubt, only clarity, we would stand like this
    forever.

Time passing on, its merry dance;
Went forth with scarce regard,
And we fought through life's adversities,
And found joy, though times were hard,
A partnership not of diamond but
Wrought as out of Iron,
Companions sharing all this world,
A mutual arm to cry on.
We stood as one with hands entwined to face the world
    together,
And I knew no doubt, only clarity, we would stand like this
    forever.

Our foundations were as oak,
Deep roots from aging tree,
And fate, or chance, or providence,
Turned our small group to three.
Our daughter, kissed by sunshine,
With all still yet to know.

Our whole world and our worries,
Life's greatest high and low.
We stood as one with hands entwined to face the world
    together,
And I knew no doubt, only clarity, we would stand like this
    forever.

Life's last cruel twist, the parting ways,
For nothing lasts forever,
And yet the strongest bonds of love,
The weakest flesh can sever.
A young girl standing by a graveside,
Trying not to cry,
And he stood, they stood, together,
And I heard them say goodbye.
They stood as one with hands entwined to face the world
    together,
And I knew no doubt, only clarity, they would stand like this
    forever.

Amiri's Revolution
Krystal Valentine

you are sweet milk stretched with water &
i am sweet milk stretched with water &
we are the recipe for overcoming
that has eluded

corporate bodies
making upper class white american love,
in beds too comfortable to creak their
lack of monotony. so,

if i am not too brown for beautiful &
you are not too brown for beautiful, then
get us war hammers
to smash the quiet cradle of the
tenderly birthed genocide of the
museum exhibit of my grandmother's hips.
the breaking news story that is your father's hands.
the zoo attraction of my hair.

is this not our nappy america?
working single mother romance flirting through
police officer kicked out teeth.
little boy skulls branded with cell numbers.
professional lips stapled shut, bleeding broken spine vernacular.
our names are tiaras with the diamonds torn out. so,

if i am not too poor for beautiful &
you are not too poor for beautiful, then
fingernail dig this gold-thirsty desire from my chest
until touch burns worse
than an overdue light bill.

until your head forgets
the way our prayers grew
overripe peach soft, realizing our words
were dust collecting
in upper class white american God's
answering machine.

My Mother Has No Teeth
Jennifer Lowers Warren

My Mother Has No Teeth

She thinks she is now marked
by age—somehow less beautiful.

She doesn't realize that her mouth,
empty, is just another sign of her self-sacrifice.
Her lovers, her elasticity and now
her teeth are all offerings,
more significant than wheat or lambs.

Her hands remain out and open,
palms up, just so her children
can glisten like gods.
Teeth straight from braces,
white as doves.

Celestial Pursuit
Leah Smith

"... he saw a stairway resting on the earth,... and the angels of God were ascending and descending on it." Genesis 28:12

"Then he said, 'Let me go, for the day has broken,' But Jacob said, 'I will not let you go unless you bless me'." Genesis 32:26

Chasing the pregnant moon on four tires,
aggressive shadows labored to keep me at bay.
Heated pavement groaned, telling the truth
about me and my frantic speeds,
the lengths I was willing to go—
to the edge of earth's soul, pursuing
dim glints of dull yellow.

Unmasking the same path Jacob saw—
with no ethereal ladder;
no seraphim rising and falling;
only a chocolate sky with almonds that shined.
No divine hand hindered my hip,
wrestling me, demanding
submission as a prerequisite to His blessing.

Instead, angels played hopscotch
with cosmic rocks on dusty trails
laid by eager stars hoping for heaven
                                      with me on their tails.

The Bridge
Caren Stewart

There's a bridge on my street
and I walk towards it quickly
as I approach I see a man and a woman
standing there
leaning against the railing and I see
the woman
with bright orange hair
whom I have known in other circumstances
and she is pointing
saying look
and I see three deer
standing there silently, knowing nothing
so close I could toss stones onto
their backs

under this bridge runs a wide creek
and at times the water moves quickly
making its way around old tires
and fallen branches
dragging debris
but sometimes the water becomes stagnant
shimmering with oil rainbows
scum covering the surface
broken only where waterbugs glide

we would swim in the water
in the deeper parts
where the rocks jut out from the shore

and the undergrowth overhangs
and sometimes when we stood
there would be small black leeches
shiny and slick
clinging to our bodies
but we were mesmerized
by the sun as it patterned the water and
danced on the backs of silver colored fish

along this wide creek there runs a path
you can walk along this path and stop
to rest under this bridge where it's
all cement coolness
graffiti words are scratched hard into the smooth face
of concrete
nonsense words
meaningless words
left there by unknown people

we would stand on this path
under this bridge and listen
to our voices echoing as we sang silly songs
giggling, madly, spinning in circles
and I would be a princess
skipping around
eyes closed
falling onto the soft silt lining the path

but this day I am walking over this bridge
not reminiscing
walking hard and fast
there is a car over my shoulder
slowing

it's a woman that I do not know
she is pointing saying look
please, please be careful as you walk over this bridge at night
I say okay but it's not enough
please promise me that you'll be very careful
something terrible happened to a young girl
here on this bridge

Warning Label
Cait Cox

People should come with a warning label
Like: flammable, keep away from open flame
Like: fragile, handle with care
Like: stay away from the edge, because it's jagged and bare
So everybody will know what they're up against when they meet someone new

Children learn that stoves are hot
And knives are sharp
But we run with scissors grasped in our burnt palms from touching the stove eye anyway
Humans have a tendency for destruction
Self-inflicted or otherwise
And that all comes with a long list of things that we tend to keep away from prying eyes
Call it entropy, or whatever you like,
And maybe if we had a little warning
We could make better informed escape plans for those conversations we don't want to have

We should come warning labels
Like: I'm broken
Or
Please don't touch
Like: take me in moderation because I know I can be too much

Pick me out like a prescription pill from your drug shelf,
Make sure you read the side effects and information that is usually thrown in the trash
I promise to be honest with you,
Because the bad things are part of me too

But maybe people don't come with warning labels
For the same reason we don't come with expiration dates
We all know we have them
But live to keep the mystery alive
See, maybe we need to get to know ourselves and be more gracious with our flaws
You should not love yourself despite, but because of

Learn to be more willing to put your fractured pieces out on the table
Build a stained glass window from all the shattered parts
We all share this thing called existence, it's never perfect
Neither are we
Teach children

Not to wear warning labels like:
Caution! Flammable
But rather that
It's ok to blow up sometimes,
Then help them put themselves back together
Read the danger signs and the benefits back to back
Although
We need to see the good bits are all wrapped up with the bad ones
But neither one makes us more or less than who we are
We are more than a warning label

If We Knew
Mike Wilson

You sit there in the homeless camp,
legs propped up with a casual air;
Or walk the roadside with a sign,
Just needing enough sustenance,
however you define that...

You have a significant story,
each and every one of you.

Especially the veterans of foreign wars...
Thrust onto improbable kill-zones at a
still-delicate age, hardened on the outside.
Decades later you still bear the scars.

If we knew the horrors you witnessed,
the debacles and disasters you participated in;
If we could be there at every atrocity
committed by both sides, and remember.

Understanding might dawn on us,
what we unwittingly helped support,
why things had to be the way they did,
how someday they might be different.

But we do not know, and so we may just
wave, or ignore you, or throw some coins.
Forgive the ignorance of those you defended,
For they know not the price that was paid.

Senior Winners
2013–2014

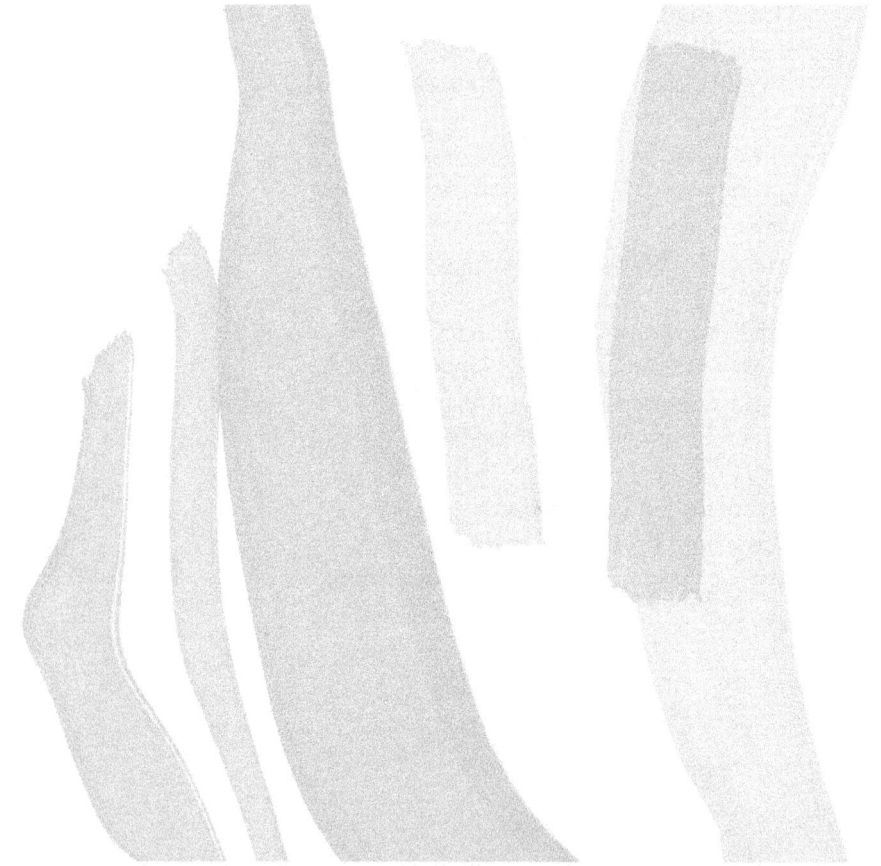

Do You Know Me?
Daniel George

Look at me if you can, if you dare, I am, I am your enemy.
You cannot fix your sights on me
From the twin PETRONAS towers in Malaysia, Nor from the luxury condo of Manhattan,
You will neither see me when you are basking in the Caribbean sun in a beach resort,
But I am the enemy; I am everywhere, dwelling throughout our planet.

On the trash mounds of the Favelas of S" o Paulo Brazil, the ghettos of Soweto,
The streets of Kolkata, under the bridges or on the sidewalks of Cambodia,
Can you see me searching for an aluminum can, plastic bag or pieces of paper?
To fetch me a dollar from the recycler?
I am dwelling on the trash heaps in search of a morsel of food,
Rotten bananas and tomatoes, bits of chicken meat clinging to the chewed pieces,
Valuable life sustainers in my world.

I will wait for you to find me; I am busy protecting my baby sister
From the pedophiles, drug pushers and pimps as much as I can.
Most of the times I am too frail and cannot fight against a force so evil and strong, alone.
My tummy is hungry always craving for food;
I am stricken with malnourishment and sickness,
Lots of folks fight us every day in this world
We see choppers hovering over us dropping packets of dried meals,
Our frail hands stretched and sunken eyes staring to catch those packets

You cannot hear the cries of by brothers and sisters from where you stay,
You can never see my baby brother's pleading eyes and tear streaked dirty cheeks
Come near, look closer and listen vigilantly, if you really want to find and fight me.
    YES! I am your enemy and my name is "POVERTY"

You will face me one day somewhere: You then will answer—in unspoken words:
Trying to retreat to the cozy world of yours, not ready and armed to fight against me,
 Or is it because you don't want to fight? I am the enemy who can be fierce if let loose;
Time will tell when we will be—*Monstrous enough to make this world shudder with fear;*
Ignore me not "Hey Mankind" we are all around you.
Ignore me not. I am your true enemy.

The Diagnosis
Ruth Merriman

It wasn't supposed to be me,
The one in perfect health,
Zipping around
While others are down with the flu.
Never me.

It can't possibly be me,
The poster girl for older folks,
Still hiking at eighty-one,
Stronger than some half my age.
Not me.

Now I'll be the one lagging behind
Shuffling along,
Trembling and shaking.
Trapped in my body's betrayal.
Why me?

But logic has no bearing
On the whimsies of disease,
Its victims chosen by some secret lottery,
Indiscriminately.
Yes, it's me.

An Artist Remembered
Roger Brock

An artist is never really gone
Her works live on, have a life of their own
Her life story is found in the colors on the canvas
Part of herself left with each painting
Along with her signature
An artist pours her soul into her paintings
Chooses the colors so carefully
Capturing beauty in the world
An artist's life is framed with beauty

An artist is never really gone
Her studio may be empty now
Except for the palette left behind
With yesterday's colors
And dried paint and brushes nearby
Her paintings tell her story
They reflect who she was
And her life's experiences
An artist pours her soul into her paintings

An artist is never really gone
Left in her friends' memories
Her loving family will always remember
the many hours painting a scene,
getting it right, getting it on paper, her own mark
Artists are special gifted people,
Giving more than they receive
Pouring their souls into their paintings

An artist is never really gone
A painting of hers will remind you
of her unique style, her colorful life

Her desire to put what she sees on paper for all to see
To capture the joy of the moment
Like a snapshot in time
Stopping the clock for a second
For a view of the world from the artist's eyes

An artist is never really gone
Don't look for her at the gravesite
Find her instead in the flowers in the meadow
On the canvas where she left so much of herself
And her view of this beautiful world

In the end, isn't Life like a painting
When the breath is gone,
it becomes a still life
Here on Earth at least

But Life lives on in Heaven we believe
Yes, look for her with Heaven's angels
That walk among us
Guiding an artist's hand
To create beauty in this earthly world
An artist's soul is in her paintings

Little Things
Joan Lacombe

It's little things that make life grand
A smile, a tear, a wedding band
Honey buns and daffodils
The sun shining on faraway hills.

Moon and stars to brighten the night
Watching a graceful bird in flight.
The grace notes in the music adding style
To the melody that makes human life worthwhile.

Small unremembered acts of human kindness
Make life sweet, beautiful, and together bind us.
Little deeds are the mortar that hold the world together
Giving order and meaning to make our lives better.

Little things count, our lives they clarify
Who we really are, they identify.
Little things serve the Lord of all existence
Rewarding us for faith, loyalty and persistence.

The small stones that great cathedrals make
Where God is worshiped; He does not forsake.
Little things will be remembered, unflawed
Like stars in the crowns of all the saints of God.

A smile, a touch can mean so much.
A card, a note, a letter can make someone feel better.
A kind word, a listening ear
An honest compliment, so sincere.

A simple act of caring,
Someone's sadness sharing.
All have the potential to turn a life around
Assuring that happiness will abound.

I may not be capable of great things
But I can surely do little things.
Nothing to debate; no time to hesitate,
It's time for me to start doing my part.
No better time than right now!

Father
Mark Littleton

Cigar smoke and him up to his knees
in the river, casting flies.
Him yelling orders and laughing
as we screamed for a strike.

Him tying a bowline
and showing us how—taking our fingers
and guiding them with his rough hands
until we got it.

Him pulling out a blade of grass,
putting it between his thumbs
and blowing; making that sound.
What was that sound?

Him in the yard, leaning on a rake
and laughing; us tumbling in the leaves
and him pitching the pile on us,
burying us. Then all of us burying him,
and laughing,
laughing.

Him sitting at the table,

poring over the books.
Mom telling him it would work out.
Somehow it would work out.

Him on his knees by the bed
each morning, murmuring; his face
in his hands, his shoulders bent.

Then the long dry seasons
and him pleading with the sky
and God.

Him plodding home each day
and stumbling on the hardened clumps
of dirt.

Then the last drought, everything
burned out. And him out behind the barn,
his back against the slats,
one hand gripping dust,
the other a gun.

Finally, the blast
that I still hear every day,
even now, at sixty.

Him never knowing
that I saw.

The Tale of Emmett Till
Gordon Smith

Did you know my sweet li'l boy
Who loved to laugh and play?
He was a mother's pride and joy.
Why did he die that way?

He went from home to see his kin
In Mississippi land;
He played a game with friends and then
He told them of his plan.

Into the store he bravely went
And sought to buy a toy;
He seemed to lose his sense
Like any other boy.

He flirted with a woman fair
And tried to hold her hand.
She cringed, and with a wounded air
She ran to tell her man.

That night he lay in bed awake,
Afraid, and so alone.
He knew not why, what course to take,
His heart as cold as stone.

Two men in white approached his bed
And stole my boy away;
They beat him, cursed him, bruised his head,
All night, till light of day.

The river cold became his tomb,
Weighed down with bands of steel;
My boy who loved me from the womb
No one but Heaven could heal.

His skin so dark, his race, his kind,
Had set him far apart—
Too far for wicked men to find
The goodness in his heart.

Until the day when right prevails,
When we are all the same,
There'll always be just one more tale,
No matter what the name.

Did you know my sweet li'l boy
Who loved to laugh and play?
He was a mother's pride and joy.
Why did he die that way?

Out of the Wild
David M. Harris

Sound ricochets through the valley,
across the river, bank to bank.
From the porch, you hear the wails
that sound at first like sirens.
The dog rises, nervous, and sniffs,
and stays close. He knows
his cousin's call. Just beyond Manhattan's
night-time glow, coyotes haunt these hills.
In the morning, you grab the train for Grand Central,
while wildness sleeps in your backyard.

Weight
Joan Cannon

I should have known ashes aren't light.
Velvet wrapped around a box that needs
both my hands to lift.
How could it be so heavy?

How to set down this burden? Where?
As if inside is something unique,
I carry it tenderly, reverently...
without a sound escaping my throat.

Remember this coda is universal.
I place it behind a cupboard door.
On what scale do we weigh the contents?
Even in ashes the true heft of a soul is left behind.

Yesterday
Sarah Bailey

    Yesterday
I remembered when you were just a whisper in the night.
A thought not yet conceived
Until I felt you flutter, like butterfly wings
In silence of a moment.
That day a long time ago.
It seems like yesterday

    Yesterday
I remembered the first time I saw your face.
Counted all your little toes
It was love at first glance
Captured, enslaved by your innocents
My life forever changed
It seems like yesterday

    Yesterday
I remembered your first smile
Your first tooth
Your first awkward steps
Beginnings of journeys away from me
Exploring unknown worlds
It seems like yesterdays

    Yesterday
I remembered meeting your new love
Seeing the happiness on your wedding day
I remember the joy of a new little life
The wonder of watching you, with your precious babe
The thrill of being a new Grandma
It seems like yesterday

    Yesterday
I remembered my youth
Now my hair has turned to silver
My skin has lost its youthful glow
My steps have gotten slower
But I will always remember
The miracle of YOU!

Assassins in Time
Nancy Culp

They come, twisted shadows
murderous eyes watching, waiting
biding their time, these assassins,
destroyers of tomorrow
pirates of time.

See those fleeting black flashes
through the corner of your eye?
Tiny beetles skittering under the bed?
A stray fleck of mascara perhaps?
Do we fear they are demons,
wicked spirits hungry for a taste
of fresh soul

Or do we kneel before the Holy See
of modern medical science?
If we have read enough Stephen King

under the covers at midnight
Dean Koontz? Edgar Allen Poe?
then we will understand.
We've become familiar with shadows.

No moral or ethical consideration
here. These assassins are simply
executing their primordial assignments
gathering strength to one day ambush
our unsuspecting cells
compromised immune systems
and detonate their bomb-filled SUVs.

Oh, we can attempt to divert them
postpone their deadly missions
invalidate their obsessive Jihad
with our positive lifestyle adjustments
billion dollar pharmaceutical industry
    antioxidants

But we cannot defeat these creators and nurturers of our
    pathology,
these ancient suicide bombers slowly destroying themselves
as they destroy us.
Well, do your work assassins.
We will not waste our time for
the simple fear of losing it, or bow
our heads in timorous anticipation
of your inevitable victory. We have
only now; this moment; this day.

Tomorrow
is always a presumption.

Loved and Cared
Carmen Ruelas Von Tickner

We once walked together
We once talked and shared
We once knew each other
When we both loved and cared

Moments filled with bliss
Moments filled with tears
We both had each other
When we both loved and cared

From worlds so far apart
we found a common ground
To reach and teach each other
When we both loved and cared

Now the curve of life is bending
Like the branches of a tree
With all the scattered thoughts
Falling on a darken sea

The loudness of your silence
Now echoes through my mind
With each passing day it seems
We no longer love or care

I Am A Poem
Jerome E. Howard

I am Morning's First Light and Twilight's Last Remains.
I am the Happiness in Change and the Joy in "Just the Same."
I am Destiny's Knock and Opportunity's Open Door.
I am the Smell of Spring and Fall's Desire to be More.

I am the Reality of Now and the Best of Past "Whens."
I am the Freshness of Youth and the Wish to begin again.
I am an Older Age and the Wisdom to be Shared.
I am a Life Alone and Another to be Paired.

I am You and Me and Everyone in Between.
I am Light and Darkness...the Seen and the Unseen.
I am Time Rushing Rapidly and the Clocks Steady Path.
I am Words and Sounds and Truth That Will Last…...I Am A Poem....

The Tally Of Time
Robert B. Robeson

They had their time…but it was long ago,
    and now their smiles are like sunrise
    on a sea littered with wreckage,
casual relics of antiquity left alone
    upon some distant shore, to
gather rust and be neglected.

Idols of today…tired from ceaseless excitement,
    pushing the heroes of yesterday out of
    mind or recollection,
engrossed in the present and uncaring of those
    who gave meaning to the past,
watching history fade into fable.

Earth, a place of graves…the heavens a hope,
    their tracks in life strewn with the
    embers from dimming fires,
so soon forgotten, like waves washing
    their imprints from the sand,
their monuments becoming ruins.

Being old is time…silently turning its pages,
    while youth disdainfully tries to toss
    them by the wayside.
Someday *their* time will also come
    to face the lonely nights.
The pangs are sharp, yet unavoidable.

Other Project Anthologies

Poetry Matters Anthology
Power of Words
Poetry Diversified
Poetry Diversified 2015

Judges 2013–2014

Donna Weir-Soley was born and raised in Jamaica. She currently teaches at Florida International University as an Assistant Professor in the English Department. She is a poet, critic, and has been published in six journals, and anthology *Moving Beyond Boundaries*. She also published her poetry book, *First Rain*, in 2006.

Jeska Clark has been with Poetry Matters since its inception in 2000. She graduated from Arizona State University where she obtained her Bachelors of Arts degree in Communication. She volunteers as a judge for the middle school category.

R. Xavier Clark began working as assistant editor for P.R.A. Publishing in 2006. He has worked with Poetry Matters since its inception. He judged the high school category and has worked on development of the annual awards program. He received his Bachelors of Science in Consumer Economics from University of Georgia in December 2014.

Lucinda Clark is the co-founder and contest coordinator for Poetry Matters. This year, she judged the high school category. She is an award-winning publisher and founder of P.R.A. Publishing. While working to promote poetry, she has also been able to work with authors from all over the globe. Clark currently resides in Martinez, GA. Visit P.R.A. Publishing at www.prapublishing.com

J.C. Elkin is a graduate of Bates College, Southern Connecticut State University, and the Defense Language Institute. Founder of The Broadneck Writers' Workshop, she is the author of "World Class: Poems Inspired by the ESL

Classroom," as well as numerous prize-winning poems and prose works. She works as a language teacher, theater critic and singer, and makes her home on the Chesapeake Bay. She will be our Mistress of Ceremonies this year.

Takisha Perry published her first poetry book titled *When She-Motions Hit the Page*, along with two books entitled *Woman's Heart Journey and Out of the Mouth of Babes*, and *Truth Speaketh*. Perry is the founder and president of the Inspiring Literary Group "For PASSION Authors."

Pauline Findlay was born in Trinidad, West Indies and migrated to the United States as a small child. Findlay wrote her first work of poetry entitled "Wind Song", at the age of 14. She wouldn't write again formally for sixteen years. Since then Findlay has written and compiled a large collection of poetic selections and short stories, that encompass a range of lifestyles, social behaviors, and cultural mores. Her book *Mirror Images* was released in 2012. She can be found lighting up the Brooklyn poetry circuit with Rimes of The Ancient Mariner.

Ira E. Harrison a.k.a. Dr Poet is President of the Georgia Poetry Society. He received his Bachelor Degree at Morehouse College, his Master Degree at Atlanta University, his Ph.D. at Syracuse University, and his Masters of Public Health at John Hopkins University. He has published six books of poetry.

Sheema Kalbasi was born November 20, 1972 in Tehran, Iran. She is an award winning poet, producer and the founder and president of Reel Content, a film production and publishing company. Kalbasi is the director and the co-director of several literary projects including the Other Voices International Project. Her poems have been anthologized and translated into eighteen languages to date. Kalbasi's work is distinguished by her passionate defense of minorities' rights. She has done voluntary teaching and tutoring of Baha'i refugee children as well as Iraqi Kurdish children, and disadvantaged Pakistani children in Pakistan. Kalbasi has worked for the United Nations and the Center for Refugees in Pakistan, and in Denmark. She lives in Washington, D.C. with her husband and children.

Sharon Schroeder is a longtime member of the Fort Gordon "family" said she began writing as a child and had a neighborhood storytelling club "creating and telling stories on the front porch while other kids were running around playing cops and robbers. "She is a graduate of the University of Arkansas, where she majored in Speech Communication and Drama. She later earned a teaching certificate and another degree in English from the University of Central Arkansas. She published her poetry memoir on her travels as a military wife, *Saltwaters Blues*. She currently teaches English at Augusta Technical College.

NC Weil prefers the elbow room of novels to the restricted arc of short stories, and she blogs at http://aestheticpoint.blogspot.com/. Her fiction has appeared in the anthology *Electric Grace* (Paycock Press, 2007) and the online journal ArLiJo. Her novels follow characters through pockets of counterculture in the late seventies, when psychedelics were a sacrament and so much seemed possible.

Acknowledgements

With every passing year this section is becoming the best part in completing the anthology project. There are so many people to thank for making this book and our growing contest possible year after year.

I would like to first thank our sponsors; Center for Primary Care has provided cash prizes since the contests inception in 2000, and the Aiken Standard has been a steadfast supporter. I would also like to say thank you to P.R.A. Publishing for providing the muscle that keeps things on track.

We simply could not make the Poetry Matters Lit Prize possible without our dedicated judges. For 2013-2014 judging we had: Jessica and Lucinda Clark who judged the middle school category. We utilized the skills of Xavier Clark, Pauline Findlay, and Sharon Schroeder for the high school category. For the adult category, NC Weil, Sheema Kalbasi, Takisha Perry and Donna Weir-Solei were kind enough to be judges. Deanna Shapiro, Gina Bahr, J.C. Elkin and Ira Harrison, PhD, worked hard on the senior category.

Last but not least, I must thank my assistant Rashida Weedon for keeping this anthology on track and Joe Tantillo who completed the cover and layout for this anthology. As always, we could not do what we do if you didn't do what you do!

www.ingramcontent.com/pod-product-compliance
Lightning Source LLC
Chambersburg PA
CBHW051657040426
42446CB00009B/1183